"*Spirited Leadership* excites me because of the simple way it reveals the characteristics and traits that build trust, respect, and dignity, not just at work but in the way we live our lives. It is rich with gems of truth in every section along with the opportunity to evaluate our current behavior and the challenge to become a *spirited* leader, not just a manager or a leader. As an experienced participant in Ellen's workshops, I can say that *Spirited Leadership* captures the essence of Ellen, and I will read this book again and again."

>—COSBY M. DAVIS III,
> Chief Financial Officer and Treasurer,
> PARTNERS National Health Plans of North Carolina

"A fascinating and imaginative book, this is surely our best hope for living more humanly."

>—THOMAS H. GROOME,
> Professor of Theology and Education,
> Boston College

"*Spirited Leadership* goes beyond describing effective management and leadership characteristics. Ellen provides practical "how-to's" for enhancing and implementing essential leadership skills."

>—PAULA HILL,
> Director, Business Leadership Center
> Edwin L. Cox School of Business
> Southern Methodist University

"Ms. Castro's view of leadership drives directly to the heart of the issue: Leadership based upon the principles of trust and integrity all within the context of who we are as spiritual human beings. Her *Reflections* are insightful and useful in helping to create change in both ourselves and others as leaders in the world today."

>—DAVID L. GONZALES,
> Vice President,
> Frito-Lay International

"Ellen Castro's beliefs that we reap what we sow, and that relationships of trust, not money, are the measure of success, are both practical and divinely authorized. Her 52 ways really work."

—CHRISTOPHER STONE,
Author of *Re-Creating Your Self*

"*Spirited Leadership* will help leaders define the culture necessary to build a truly successful and fulfilling business . . . Ellen Castro has given us clear goals to strive for."

—CARL SEWELL,
Author of *Customers for Life* and
Chairman of Sewell Motor Company

"Embracing the traits and behaviors identified in *Spirited Leadership* will undoubtedly make a dramatic difference not only at work but in the community itself."

—FRANK DAVILA II,
Chief Attorney for Bexar County Justice Center,
San Antonio, Texas

"*Spirited Leadership* is enlightening and to the point. I will use the book a week at a time with my employees. I can now see how part of my success has evolved, but better yet, I see much room in my own workplace for improvement."

—DENNIS NOVOSEL,
President, Stoney Creek Furniture
Stoney Creek, Ontario
1998 Education Chairman of the
National Home Furnishings Association

Spirited LEADERSHIP

52 ways to build TRUST on the job

ELLEN CASTRO

ThomasMore®
– An RCL Company –
Allen, Texas

Book cover and inside design by:
Melody Loggins, Zia Designs

Section dividers contain original artwork by Ellen Castro. Artwork for
"Cultivates a Climate for Success" and "Instills a Sense of Community"
was inspired by artist Anthony D'Agostino.

All quotes appearing in *Spirited Leadership* have been collected by
the author over the years from various books, television programs,
magazines, and periodicals.

Send all inquiries to:

Thomas More
An RCL Company
200 East Bethany Drive
Allen, Texas 75002-3804

Toll Free: 800-264-0368
Fax: 800-688-8356

Visit our website at **www.rclweb.com**

Printed in the United States of America

ISBN 0-88347-363-1

1 2 3 4 5   02 01 00 99 98

Dedicated with
love and gratitude to

E. B. CASTRO, JR.

Special Thanks

❖ To each and every individual who has participated in my classes and workshops . . . for the learnings, love, and reality checks.

❖ To Alyson Cate and John Jones . . . clients, partners, and friends since the inception of Effectiveness Consulting.

❖ To Ken Blanchard, Stephen R. Covey, James M. Kouzes, and Barry Z. Posner . . . their workshops and works impacted my way of being.

❖ To Debby Singleton and other teachers and authors . . . for sharing their wisdom and knowledge.

❖ To Bill Linburg . . . for my "oldest" friendship, the encouragement, and computer skills.

❖ To Debra Hampton . . . a gifted and gracious editor.

❖ To my clients . . . for their belief in my talent and work.

❖ To my family and friends . . . for the gifts of spirit, love, compassion, forgiveness, and joy.

❖ To my angel, Faith . . . for faith has set me free.

Contents

Honors Self

Cherishes Values

Acts Truthfully and Honestly

Exudes Competence

Behaves Courteously

Radiates Confidence and a Positive Attitude

Lives the Talk

Takes Themselves Lightly

Acts with Humility

Expresses Passion

Honors Others

Serves

Shoots Straight

Instills Self-Worth

Expects the Best in Others

Is Compassionate

Listens with Ears, Eyes, and Heart

Allows Others to Become Self-Reliant

Promotes Creativity and Curiosity

Thinks Before Speaks or Acts

Is Forgiving and Gracious

Embodies Fairness

Recognizes and Affirms

PREFACE

Fascinating, it was easier writing this book than this brief preface. My editor suggested I include this reality.

The reality is that I gave up my spirit and soul at work.

It was not intentional, yet the ramifications and consequences were the same.

I so much wanted success and approval that I did whatever it took to gain it. I do not look back at this time proudly, but it was the only behavior I knew and for the most part modeled. I did not honor myself and ignored my inner knowing.

However, at age 32, I was making a great salary ($55,000+) and had earned four weeks' vacation in the early 1980s. Yet, with all the outward success and position, inside I was emotionally dying. Inwardly, I felt empty and did not like what I had become: a person of lost integrity. Money and success were my God.

I had acquired many material things but was experiencing emptiness and a lack of inner peace and joy. Eventually, the continual denial of my spirit and soul led to a major illness. In hindsight, what a blessing!

This experience led me to learn more about myself and others. I found that as I honored myself, I was truly capable of honoring others. The relationships that occurred were bountiful and nurturing. These relationships were based on trust and compassion and generated feelings of worth, confidence, and esteem. Subsequently, I was free to become my best self.

It has been a phenomenal revelation: the ability to find trust, joy, and prosperity on the job, at home, and in the community.

Now 13 years later, my life is unequivocally more joyful, happy, peaceful, and prosperous than ever before. My life is filled with riches, both intrinsic and external.

I thank God and spirit from the bottom of my heart for my path. Without knowing such emptiness, I would not be aware of such abundance.

The way of spirit provides a better and easier path. This path shows us that if we believe and trust in ourselves, we can believe and trust in others. In essence, we reap what we sow.

"We were born to make manifest the glory of God within us.
It is in everyone, and as we let our own light shine,
we give other people permission to do the same."

Nelson Mandela

Introduction

Sow much, reap much.
Sow little, reap little.
Chinese Proverb

It is so simple . . . reap what you sow. It makes sense. It parallels natural laws. It is not complicated.

But if this is true, why does it seem that creating trust at work is such a challenge? Could it be that we forget who we are: children of God, spiritual beings? Could it be that we put on a mask in our role of boss, manager, or teacher and forget our true nature and the nature of those we lead?

Life does not have to be so overwhelming and complex if we keep it simple. We should treat others the way we want to be treated . . . always.

Every action as a leader sends a message. Every action either adds to or takes away from our credibility and the lives of the people we lead. There are no neutral actions. We know this but forget amid the chaos, change, and demands of today's world.

We forget that we cannot live our lives alone. Our success and the success of those we lead is measured by our relationships.

"Are you crazy?" you say. "We all know that true success is measured by money and what we acquire financially, socially, and professionally."

But I do not believe this to be true. I believe that healthy, caring, inspiring relationships create passion and commitment, which result in a healthy life and true success. We also regain the gifts of the spirit, on which no price can be placed.

Think back. When were you at your best? When did you want to achieve the impossible? What characteristics and behaviors did your best leader display? During these times, we and our leaders were influenced by the basic law of cause and effect: reap what you sow . . . a natural life cycle.

This book is written as a reminder of what we know and feel inherently: as I treat others, they will treat me. As I care for others, they will care for me. As I serve others, they will serve me. As I help others grow, they will help me to grow.

The process and results will be a gift from God—not heartache, drama, and pain. At times we may experience these aspects but not consistently.

This book is written from my heart. I have been there: the struggle to succeed, prove my worth, and to be No. 1. And I made it! But what a toll it took on my soul. Now my life is simpler, more joyous, and so much more abundant, both tangibly and intangibly. There is a God who is with us always. And remembering who we are 24 hours a day makes a difference. It does not serve us to be "two" people—one at home and another at work.

Throughout this book, I will reference values, principles, and truths. The reference is to higher truths and morally sound values. These truths and values are based on love and service and are for our higher good and the benefit of the community.

This book is about relationships: sound, nurturing relationships built on trust. Trust is based on exhibited behaviors. Actions speak louder than words.

These 52 behaviors are meant as guides to create, grow, or re-establish trust in our lives. As we create healthier, more trusting relationships, we can provide healing in all aspects of our communities and souls.

We are all one. As we treat others, we will be treated. As we lead others, they will lead. God bless. Enjoy the journey. Open your hearts to the possibilities. May you reap . . .

trust

respect

laughter

joy

accomplishment

harmony

wholeness

profits at work

and wealth in your life!

CORE BELIEFS

*A little consideration, a little thought
for others, makes all the difference.*
Winnie the Pooh

These are core beliefs that underlie my thoughts in writing this book:

❖ Every human is afforded dignity.

❖ Service involves giving of ourselves to others.

❖ Self-integrity is necessary.

❖ There is no failure, only learnings and lessons.

❖ Trusting our inner knowing is healthy.

❖ Every action impacts our relationship with self, others, and the community.

❖ There are no neutral acts; they either add to or take away from our credibility.

❖ Surrendering to the grace of God reduces stress.

❖ Balance in all areas is key.

❖ Every moment we can be in love, service, or fear. It is our choice.

❖ We are all interconnected through the One Source.

Spirited LEADERSHIP

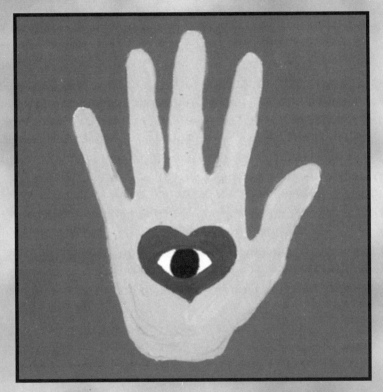

Honors Self

Honors Self

Love the Lord thy God with all thy heart,
with all thy soul, and with all thy mind.
And love thy neighbor as thyself.
Deuteronomy 6:5; Matthew 22:37–39

Honoring self sets the foundation. To honor others and be a selfless leader, you must first honor yourself. You cannot give to others what you cannot give to yourself.

Unless you honor yourself, your actions will not originate from integrity. Your actions will be in the guise of a "people person" leader in which you are trying to please and gain acceptance and approval. Or worse, because you do not honor yourself, why honor anyone else?

How can you lead others until you lead yourself? How can you be fair to others when you are unfair to yourself? How can you delight in others' power and gifts when you feel threatened or fearful because you have not realized and honored your gifts and personal power?

It is simple. To truly honor others, one must begin by honoring self.

REFLECTIONS

Do you believe it is okay and in fact healthy to have boundaries?

_____

_____

_____

If no, why not? Are you afraid of losing something or someone? If so, what?

_____

_____

_____

If yes, list the boundaries you choose to live life by. Are they out of love and respect for yourself or out of fear?

_____

_____

_____

CHERISHES VALUES

Try not to become a person of success,
but rather a person of value.
Albert Einstein

Leaders are consciously aware of the values and principles by which they live their lives. They integrate these values and principles professionally and personally. Through constant choice, they remain faithful to their truths, their values, and themselves. Even in today's dynamic environment, they are able to care about others because their identities are secure. With this value-based decision making, they bring meaning and integrity in their roles as leaders, personally and professionally. They experience no separation of self. This is true success.

As a result, the people they lead feel safe to bring all their talents and gifts to bear.

Integrity is knowing and living your values. Integrity is the foundation for leadership and trust. How can you have integrity if you do not know for what you stand? How can you be untruthful and dishonest but expect truthfulness and honesty from others? And most importantly, how can you lead others until you lead yourself?

Living your values enables you to maintain a whole core. Outside influences are just that . . . influences. The leader can view the influences objectively and ask, "Is there a better way? Will this aid in my development and leadership?"

Take the time now to write and articulate your values and principles. Acknowledge them, honor them, and celebrate them, for that is who you truly are.

Truth and integrity do have a place in all aspects of our lives.

REFLECTIONS

Are you whole? Do you feel that the person at work and the person portrayed at home are the same . . . integrated?

_____
_____
_____

List the values you hold most dear . . . the values from which you do not sway.

_____
_____
_____

What actions do you exhibit which reflect these values?

_____
_____
_____

ACTS TRUTHFULLY AND HONESTLY

The late golf champion Babe Didrikson Zaharias once disqualified herself from a golf tournament for having hit the wrong ball out of the rough. "But nobody would have known," a friend told her. "I would have known," Babe replied.

Babe Didrikson Zaharias

Once your actions are based on strong values, truthfulness becomes easy. The truth flows from the heart, not the ego. Honesty is forthright, gentle, and easily accepted. It is not masked by wanting approval. Actions originate from integrity, self approval, and well-being.

Do you trust people who are untruthful, people who say one thing and do another, or people who are brutally honest?

A person with integrity has no need to be brutally honest. Because the core is solid, they have little need for one-upmanship or proving someone wrong. For them, it is simply a matter of speaking truth. The intent of the communication changes from, "I am right, you are wrong," to "This is my truth, help me better understand yours so we can grow." The honesty is from a source of love, not fear.

This type of honesty creates an environment of nurturing, growth, and commitment. Everyone is allowed the freedom to be honest and honored. The result is a safe and kind environment in which creativity is fostered, ideas flow, and competition is left behind.

REFLECTIONS

What do honesty and truthfulness mean to you? Are there degrees of honesty? How honest are you with yourself? Do you face your greatest challenges? Hopes? Dreams?

_____

_____

_____

Are you honest with others? Or "kinda" honest depending on the circum-stances? Have there been times when you misled others or left information out? Why? Did you do this to be liked, avoid conflict, or play it safe?

_____

_____

_____

EXUDES COMPETENCE

Well done is better than well said.
Benjamin Franklin

Competence gives the leader credibility. How can a leader lead if there is no understanding of the overall purpose? How secure can followers feel if there is a lack of substance and knowledge behind the vision? How can the leader select competent team members?

Competence is broader than expertise. A leader's understanding of the goal to be achieved reaches beyond the task and includes the framework and processes for achieving success. Leaders are cognizant of their capabilities and know when to call in others to integrate the collective strengths of the group members.

Leaders' competence shows when they are able to substantiate their position by demonstrating their knowledge and thought processes. These abilities build credibility and inspire confidence. Most importantly, these abilities are valuable mentoring tools. By helping their group members better understand all aspects of the task at hand, they are building the intellectual capacity of the group. Increased brain capacity leads to more confident team players, better decisions, and increased commitment to continuous improvement.

A person of competence values and delights in watching others grow. A competent leader is always learning and growing.

REFLECTIONS

Are you confident in your skills and abilities? What are your special gifts and talents?

_____

_____

_____

Are people aware of your competence? How do you communicate your skills to others?

_____

_____

_____

In what ways do you share your gifts with others? Do you do so freely?

_____

_____

_____

BEHAVES COURTEOUSLY

*Wherever there is a human being,
there is an opportunity for kindness.*

Seneca

Common courtesy works miracles. A simple "please" and "thank you" acknowledges individuals and their contributions. Many of us caught in a chaotic environment might ask, "Why should I? My staff gets paid. That should be reward enough." My question in return would be, "How do you feel when people take your efforts for granted?" Perhaps it's acceptable for your efforts to be taken for granted occasionally, but as a steady diet?

Lack of appreciation leads to starvation of the spirit and a loss of enthusiasm. The end result is a decline in initiative, creativity, and productivity.

Does common courtesy take much effort?

Once as I traveled across the country implementing a new program, I asked employees to tell me one action that management could take that would dramatically impact morale. Amazingly, a vast majority responded, "Common courtesy."

If we believe in and treat others with respect, their spirits soar. They begin to believe that what they do makes a difference. They begin shifting their focus from getting by to doing their best. Their efforts soon become the result of collaboration rather than competition.

This collaboration is founded on trust and achieving personal best by sharing individual gifts freely. Competition and looking over the shoulder are replaced by trust, support, and camaraderie. Life is good. Business, schools, and community prosper.

REFLECTIONS

Are "please" and "thank you" words in your vocabulary? If so, how often do you use them?

_____

_____

_____

Do you usually address people in the hallways and elevators? Do you acknowledge their presence?

_____

_____

_____

When was the last time you introduced yourself to someone whose name you did not know?

_____

_____

_____

RADIATES CONFIDENCE AND
A POSITIVE ATTITUDE

Joy comes from using your potential.
Will Schultz

When leaders honor themselves, they radiate self-respect and confidence. Confidence results in more confidence.

Genuine confidence supports a positive attitude demonstrated toward life, outcomes, and others. The positive attitude sees no failure, only feedback. It allows creation of a new path, idea, or resolution.

A leader is a person first. Their tasks become not only who they are but what they do. Risk-taking, innovation, and respecting others is easy. They first respect people for who they are and then for what they bring to the group.

A positive attitude grounded in respect and trust is contagious. Confidence and optimism radiate throughout and change is seen as good—as a chance for learning. As the leader projects self-respect, confidence, and a positive attitude, they are perceived as winners. Winners attract winners and prosperity. Imagine an organization of winners. Imagine the success.

REFLECTIONS

Are you happy with your work? Do you like doing what you are doing? How do you feel about your life in general?

_____

_____

_____

Are you generally optimistic? Do you expect the best outcome? Or are you always waiting for the shoe to drop? Could your outlook possibly affect the way you approach opportunities?

_____

_____

_____

Do you see the sun or the clouds?

_____

_____

_____

LIVES THE TALK

Example is not the main thing influencing others.
It is the only thing.
Albert Schweitzer

Okay, you are clear on your values. You are honest, competent, and confident. So what? Strong leaders must portray their convictions and feelings in every action and word. Their every action validates their beliefs.

Leaders live their talk. They understand that even their silence communicates and either adds or subtracts from their credibility.

Leaders realize their credibility not only follows them but precedes them. Have you ever met someone and instantly felt at ease because this person is known as a person of integrity and collaboration? Now think of a time when the opposite was true—you met a person known for their win-lose stance. How did you feel?

This is powerful stuff. You are only in control of you. Leaders are vigilant in living their talk and modeling the behaviors they wish in others.

REFLECTIONS

When you enter a room does the energy change for the better or worse?

_____

_____

_____

How would others rate you on a scale of 1–10 *(10 being the highest):*

_____   Lives life with integrity (1–10)?

_____   Is trustworthy (1–10)?

_____   Is respected (1–10)?

_____   Respects others (1–10)?

If your rating is less than 9, what actions can you take to change others' perception of you? Have you considered asking others to rate you? Asked for their suggestions?

_____

_____

_____

TAKES THEMSELVES LIGHTLY

Angels can fly because they take themselves lightly.

G. K. Chesterton

When you have a solid foundation, you can take yourself lightly and see the humor in all situations because you feel God's love.

This love enables you to accept imperfect humanity and recognize how glorious it is. Being human is not about perfection. It is about accepting God's grace and saying "yes" to life. It is about adding more joy and laughter to your life and your job.

Doing so inspires others to do the same, to be their best, and to enjoy the journey. Taking yourself lightly enables you to laugh, play, and contribute to a common and greater good.

REFLECTIONS

The last time you made a mistake, did you beat yourself up? Did you blame others? Did you replay the incident ad nauseam? Did you become defensive?

_____

_____

_____

Or did you give yourself a break? Did you see the lesson? Did you have a good chuckle and say to yourself, "I don't need to learn that one again"?

_____

_____

_____

Did you pat yourself on the back for being human?

_____

_____

_____

ACTS WITH HUMILITY

For everyone who raises himself up will be humbled,
but anyone who humbles himself will be raised.
Luke 18:14

Humility is essential in being perceived as trustworthy. Do you trust a person who is arrogant, boastful, or narcissistic? When we sense self-grandeur in another person, we often feel an uneasiness in the pit of the stomach—an intuitive warning.

Humility is inherent in someone who realizes their strengths and talents are gifts bestowed on them by God. They know that these are gifts to be grateful for, not arrogant with. Humility acknowledges our humanness. The spirited leader is approachable and accessible.

Humble leaders view themselves as blessed and thus revere others and their gifts. With humility and awe, the leader understands that we originated from the same source regardless of fame, power, or wealth. Humility is born through the knowledge that God only sees equality.

REFLECTIONS

Are you approachable and truly accessible? Can anyone approach you? Will they feel at ease or anxious?

_____

_____

_____

Are you respected or feared?

_____

_____

_____

What is at the center of your universe?

_____

_____

_____

EXPRESSES PASSION

Individual and corporate success comes when individuals learn to tie their hearts and hands together, to use their intellects to execute their passions and not the other way around. The driver is passion and energy of the individual. The intellect respectfully must follow.

Jann Kelso

Passion ignites the soul. The spirited leader loves their work. They believe in what they are doing. They enjoy the challenges and relish each moment of service and accomplishment.

When the leader models passion, the resulting fruits of spirit are abundant: hard work, enthusiasm, commitment, and fun. With passion, energy is released to accomplish the impossible. Passion inspires and instills trust. What better way to communicate the importance of a goal and vision than with passion! With passion, roadblocks become mere inconveniences. Where there is passion, there is spirit.

Where there is spirit, there is tapped potential. Tapped potential creates a reservoir of greater potential and achievement.

A passionate and competent leader has no equal. The best and only way to invoke passion is to embody it.

REFLECTIONS

Do you love what you do? Does it bring you joy? If not, why not? What could you perhaps do to reignite the passion?

_____

_____

_____

Do you wholeheartedly believe in your product or service? In the people with whom you work? If not, what changes could you make?

_____

_____

_____

Spirited LEADERSHIP

Honors Others

HONORS OTHERS

*It is high time the ideal of success
should be replaced with the ideal of service.*
Albert Einstein

Why honor others? Because it is the right thing to do as well as a sound business practice. As leaders honor others, group members begin to see more fully their beauty as children of God. The increased awareness creates a greater sense of self-worth, which results in gifts of spirit.

Group members are happier, more confident, more creative, and innovative; they become more adaptable to change, less stressed, better risk-takers, more amiable, and more willing to share their gifts freely.

By sharing their gifts more freely, leaders and those they lead expand and increase their talents and the talents of others. These actions result in the increased intellectual capacity of the group, which is the competitive edge.

REFLECTIONS

Do you trust others? Respect them?

_____

_____

_____

Do your behavior and words validate others? Do you refer to your staff as subordinates? My group? Or by chance do you refer to them as our team, my co-workers?

_____

_____

_____

Do you respect their space? Or invade it?

_____

_____

_____

SERVES

A leader is one who serves.
Lao Tzu

A leader who serves has true power. Sometimes that truth gets lost among the ambitious, especially those attempting to succeed in the "dog eat dog world" mentality they've seen modeled on the job, in television, and films, in the media, and in books. This type of power represents domination, in which others exist to serve themselves and their goals.

Words such as "power" and "ambition" can make a gut wrench, because in these situations, there is no place for God at work.

Power is often given to others based on the position they hold rather than on who they are.

Spirited leaders are aware of who they are, not just the role they play or what they do. By focusing on the power of love, feeling, and commitment to their followers and by serving others and caring about them and their growth, these leaders awaken spirit at work. This spirit liberates people's potential, creativity, and passion.

As for ambition, the leader who serves is ambitious. These leaders are ambitious to be the best they can be and to glorify God with their gifts. They are ambitious in allowing others the freedom and dignity to be their best selves. When group members exude this type of power, they are not competing with each other; they all want to be their best and work together.

Leaders who serve cultivate trust in the workplace. They are of service to their employees, their stakeholders, their customers, and their community.

REFLECTIONS

What is your core belief about work? Is it "dog eat dog"? "The person with the most toys wins"? Or is it perhaps, "We can make a difference"?

_____

_____

_____

Are you ambitious? What does that mean to you? What would your followers say?

_____

_____

_____

Your source of power: Is it who you are or the position you hold?

_____

_____

_____

SHOOTS STRAIGHT

What you see is what you get.

Flip Wilson

The spirited leader shares information freely and openly. They understand that information is power. They know that this type of power can transform an organization into a learning machine. This type of power fuels ownership and commitment.

Spirited leaders choose not to shield their group members from the realities of the task at hand. As a result, the group members are better equipped to meet the demands of the day, the future, and to accomplish their tasks. They become better equipped to ask tough questions and seek solutions. Open sharing of the good, the bad, and the ugly implies a sense of partnership. This partnership implies that group members respect each others' knowledge and contributions. They recognize that as members of the same team, they need one another and each plays a unique role.

When did you do your best work? When were you able to contribute to your full potential? It probably was when you had all the information to make informed choices and decisions, to think outside the box.

Shooting straight and being candid are imperative in today's ever-changing climate. Truth, honesty, and the whole picture instill confidence and a spirit of collaboration while driving out fear. Having all the necessary information fosters growth, contribution, and leadership. And, it allows others to share in creating the brighter future.

REFLECTIONS

Is information shared openly and freely in your organization?

_____

_____

_____

Is there a tendency to shield people from the whole truth? If so, what is your intent? To protect? To be all knowing?

_____

_____

_____

How do you feel when you are shielded from the facts? Are you capable of making the best decisions in a vacuum?

_____

_____

_____

INSTILLS SELF-WORTH

*Nothing helps an individual more than to place responsibility
upon them and to let them know that you trust them.*
Booker T. Washington

Leaders are cognizant that all their actions and words either contribute to or diminish the self-worth of those they lead. This is quite a responsibility and is not one to be taken lightly.

Instilling confidence, self-worth, and esteem in others is critical to the success of the individual, the team, and accomplishment of the goals. Self-esteem within a group increases morale and productivity and reduces conflict.

Self-esteem promotes self analysis, which leads to learning and the unfolding of spirit. People with self esteem are less judgmental and hurtful. They are more accepting, creative, and flexible. In this dynamic world of faster, better, quicker, how can a company, a school, or community survive unless the people feel good about themselves and their work?

An employee whose core is solid is more resilient and able to adapt. They tend to be more internally driven and pursue learning.

Feelings of self esteem foster a workplace where collaboration and WIN/WIN are the norm. In this type of environment, energies are focused on the vision rather than competing with co-workers.

Instilling self worth is morally the right action and results in an organization that flourishes.

REFLECTIONS

Do you treat others with respect and courtesy? Do you trust them to do the right thing? To fulfill their work requirements?

_____
_____
_____

Do you ask for their input and use it? Say "thanks"?

_____
_____
_____

Do you acknowledge their presence in meetings and hallways?

_____
_____
_____

Do you care about them?

_____
_____
_____

EXPECTS THE BEST IN OTHERS

Confidence begets confidence.
German Proverb

Leaders who strive to do their personal best naturally expect the same of others. They believe that they reap what they sow. They believe in themselves and believe in others' inherent goodness, honesty, and desire to do their personal best . . . to make a difference. The spirited leader treats people in a manner reflective of this respectful, honoring attitude. The self-fulfilling prophecy emerges.

The self-fulfilling prophecy or "Pygmalion effect" states that people will rise to the expectations set by others' attitudes and behaviors toward them.

The leader sees and expects honesty, goodness, and capability. Followers respond with honesty, goodness, and capability. They feel and sense the trust and care. The self-fulfilling cycle occurs. When leaders believe in and treat an individual with genuine reverence, their followers' spirits can soar and fully develop, enabling them to share their talents.

REFLECTIONS

Do you expect the best in others? Or only in some?

_____

_____

_____

Do your preconceived judgments and biases affect your expectations? List your biases.

_____

_____

_____

Do you believe that people truly want to do their best and make a difference?

_____

_____

_____

Is Compassionate

If you judge people, you have no time to love them.
Mother Teresa

Compassion in the workplace? Absolutely. People want and need to be valued for who they are as a person, not merely as a worker. Compassion involves caring, understanding, and an opening of the heart.

Spirited leaders open their hearts and are vulnerable. Within their vulnerability is humanity and the rekindling of spirit. Within this type of environment, feelings are allowed, expressed, acknowledged, and understood. Feelings are our soul.

Care and empathy are expanded to love and compassion. Love and compassion replace fear and judgment. In this climate, people are free to soar and miracles occur.

REFLECTIONS

What is compassion? How does it feel? What effect does it have on relationships?

_____

_____

_____

Are you compassionate and forgiving of yourself? Of others?

_____

_____

_____

Identify a time when you were compassionate at work. What was the outcome? How did you feel?

_____

_____

_____

LISTENS WITH EARS, EYES, AND HEART

Nature has given men one tongue, but two ears,
that we may hear from others twice as much as we speak.

Epictetus

Spirited leaders listen with all their senses; they listen with ears, eyes, and heart. Leaders who recapture spirit at work take the time to be truly present with their team members. By being totally present, they gain understanding of their thoughts, attitudes, perceptions, and feelings. The greater the leaders' comprehension of the group members' frame of reference and values, the more able the leaders can serve effectively and motivate.

Listening can be difficult for a variety of reasons, such as distractions and preoccupations, style differences, or language barriers. Additionally, the mind can think twice as fast as a person can speak. Staying present is crucial to your success and for arousing the heart and spirit.

When listening, open your heart to the communication and speaker. Let go of bias and judgments. Avoid interrupting or gaining ammunition. Maintain eye contact when appropriate. Remain open-minded. Encourage the speaker. Commit time to understand. The rewards you will reap are trust, love, and commitment . . . gifts of spirit.

As a leader, listen: learn, inspire, share, take time, encourage, and nurture.

REFLECTIONS

Are you an active listener? Do you stay focused and intent on being present?

_____

_____

_____

Do you believe that everyone's ideas, thoughts, and feelings have merit? If not, why?

_____

_____

_____

Poll your team members as to your effectiveness as a listener. Adapt, add, or change three behaviors that will increase your listening skills. List these three behaviors.

_____

_____

_____

ALLOWS OTHERS TO BECOME SELF-RELIANT

Knowledge is the food of the soul.
Socrates

A leader who recaptures spirit at work applauds another's self-reliance. They are in awe of the process and ability of others to grow and take responsibility for their work. They are neither threatened nor diminished with another's success. They foster self-reliance in a healthy, nurturing way, not through fear and intimidation.

How do you help others become self-reliant? By providing information, giving the necessary tools and resources, being a sounding board, and defining parameters. The information necessary depends on where the person is in the learning curve—it could be from providing the big picture to details of a procedure and the big picture. Tools and resources can range from the time to do the work to advanced technology. When leaders serve as a sounding board, they help their team members take calculated risks and verify their thought processes.

Leaders know their time limitations. If leaders cannot be available to be the sounding board, they find a substitute coach for their team members. Additionally, the leader or coach explains the boundaries and parameters to ensure success.

The leader gives freedom with responsibility and the followers inherently feel trusted to take ownership for their work and achieve success.

REFLECTIONS

Do you foster self-reliance? Or do you perhaps believe others might not see the need for your position otherwise? And perhaps get rid of you? (As a point of reference, I've not seen that happen in 20+ years in business.)

_____

_____

_____

Do you act from a commitment or control paradigm? Which one fosters creativity and innovation?

_____

_____

_____

PROMOTES CREATIVITY AND CURIOSITY

Courage is the power to let go of the familiar.
Anonymous

The leader is constantly asking "why?" By asking "why?" in a tone of wonder rather than defense, leaders encourage exploration, invention, and curiosity. "Why?" opens the door to the mind, its thoughts, and its frame of reference.

What would happen if today you asked "why?" about your current processes, procedures, products, and services? Would the reply be "because it's always been that way." There has never been a better time to ask "why."

Leaders ask "why?" to enable the group to eliminate those processes, procedures, products, and services that no longer make sense or are unproductive.

Questioning enables the leader and the group to begin fresh with new energy and understanding. Questioning allows the leader to cultivate an environment where curiosity and creativity are the norm and all team members are encouraged to think differently or "outside the box."

The more that leaders and those they lead question the status quo, the better the results of the group's efforts. The better the efforts, the better the quality. The more pride, the more ownership, and commitment. The more commitment, the more productivity.

Curiosity and creativity are cornerstones of a learning organization that flourishes and prospers, rather than merely surviving.

REFLECTIONS

When was the last time you asked "Why?" What kind of reply did you receive? Was the person defensive?

_____

_____

_____

When asking "why" in the past, was your intent to gain information and understand the logic or to criticize?

_____

_____

_____

Identify the new concepts or designs your organization has applied lately.

_____

_____

_____

THINKS BEFORE SPEAKS OR ACTS

Judge a man by his questions rather than his answers.

Voltaire

The role of servant leader is not to be taken lightly. It is a privilege, a responsibility, and an honor. A spirited leader is aware that every word and action either has the power to uplift spirit or diminish spirit. Leaders also know that once trust and confidence are lost, they are very difficult to regain. The leader sets the tone for the entire organization . . . humility or humiliation.

The leader is constantly asking questions. Questions open communications and stimulate thought. Questions give people the benefit of the doubt and clear up assumptions. Questions are a source of information-gathering. And information-gathering fosters well-informed thoughts, decisions, and actions.

Leaders who think before they speak and act avoid reactive responses and model strong crisis management, patience, and wisdom—three sound leadership practices promoting spirit at work.

REFLECTIONS

Do you usually engage in dialogues or monologues?

_____

_____

_____

Do you ask questions to seek information and illumination?

_____

_____

_____

Do you choose your response? Do you think before speaking? Or do you give away your power?

_____

_____

_____

Is Forgiving and Gracious

There is no justice, only mercy.
The Highlander

The spirited leader is forgiving, of self and others. Leaders forgive themselves for making mistakes. They realize that without taking risks and making possible errors, neither they nor the people they lead can grow or be innovative.

Leaders do not berate themselves for communications gone awry and creating mistrust or hurt. Instead, they admit the problem, ask for forgiveness, and seek resolution. They adjust future communications with the learning.

The spirited leader embraces the concept that we are spiritual beings having a human experience. As humans, they are not perfect and are evolving to a higher consciousness of spirit. They know they are doing their best with the tools they have and seek more resources as they learn.

They give themselves some slack.

In being gracious with themselves, they can be gracious with their group members. They cannot give to others what they cannot give to themselves. When others make a mistake, leaders do not view it with contempt or take it personally. Leaders ask themselves if the team member knows another way and begin a dialogue with that person to understand their perspective through information gathering.

This method allows leaders to increase the resources of others, enabling their team members to handle situations differently and to evolve.

Admitting mistakes, looking for learning experiences, and allowing growth are byproducts of a forgiving, gracious environment.

REFLECTIONS

As a leader, do you feel you need to have all the answers in order to be trusted and respected? Do you believe you have to get it right the first time, every time? What could these behaviors be modeling?

_____

_____

_____

When was the last time you gave someone the benefit of the doubt? Forgave them? Including yourself?

_____

_____

_____

EMBODIES FAIRNESS

Have faithfulness and sincerity as first principles.

Confucius

The servant leader reflects fairness in all interactions with all people. Fairness is at the core of trust: Can I trust you to be fair with me? Can I trust you not to play favorites? Can I trust you?

Fairness is in the eye of the beholder—the group member. Fairness encompasses consistency of behavior—behaviors that can be relied on. This behavior is based on thinking and acting, rather than reacting. This behavior is grounded in core values rather than the person or situation of the moment.

Leaders can embody fairness at all times when they know who they are and for what they stand. The leader is vigilant and lives a life of integrity.

Fairness cannot exist without integrity.

REFLECTIONS

What does fairness imply to you? How is it demonstrated?

_____
_____
_____

How have you reacted in the past when you felt an injustice occurred? Did you respect the person? Did you want to do your best?

_____
_____
_____

Did it impact future dealings?

_____
_____
_____

RECOGNIZES AND AFFIRMS

We are all desperate to belong to something larger than ourselves.
"Soulful work" is where you feel you belong.
Dana Whyte

The spirited leader understands that what gets noticed and rewarded gets reinforced. Reinforcement of desired behaviors creates the new reality where trust, love, and commitment is the norm, not the exception.

Reinforcement is not an overwhelming task because it is being done with every action and word. However, this is probably an unconscious reinforcement.

Conscious reinforcement begins simply by saying "thank you." Thank you for voicing your opinion. Thank you for helping see anew. Thank you for staying until the job was finished. Thank you for the results. Thank you for discovering a way not to do things. Thank you for being straightforward. Thank you for the effort.

There are so many opportunities to say "thank you", "I noticed", or "I recognize your efforts".

People want to be noticed, recognized, and affirmed. The more specific the affirmation, the more sincere it will sound. Sincerity is crucial. Sincere affirmation is heartfelt. Manipulation, on the other hand, is toxic.

The spirited leader recognizes that behavior must be modeled to transform the workplace into a kinder, gentler, more effective reality. The transformation begins with the leader. Modeling and affirming creates and sustains the new reality, which recaptures spirit at work.

REFLECTIONS

What behaviors and attitudes are currently being reinforced?

_____

_____

_____

List what you believe are the unwritten ground rules for success in your organization.

_____

_____

_____

Ask your team members what they believe are the unwritten ground rules for success.

_____

_____

_____

Are they consistent with what you thought?

_____

_____

_____

Spirited LEADERSHIP

Cultivates a Climate for Success

PROVIDES A VISION

The soul does not think without a picture.

Aristotle

Three of the universal needs of people are fulfilled when a leader provides a vision. These three needs are: a sense of belonging, a sense of accomplishment, and a sense of recognition.

Individuals need, want, and desire to have a sense of belonging to one another and a goal worthy of their efforts. When focus and meaning are present, a team spirit naturally unfolds and exists. People feel connected to each other and the goal. A sense of accomplishment and challenge is derived from more than one source. Accomplishment is felt at three levels: self, team, and vision—"myself," "others," and "we."

In this environment, recognition for everyone and their efforts is abundant. Everyone is seen as needed. Jealousy is absent and encouragement is present. Victories and disappointments are shared.

The spirited leader takes every opportunity to communicate the vision, which is ethical, simple, and attainable. It is a vision that inspires the heart and provides clarity. With clarity and focus, the team experiences excitement, buy-in, and commitment.

REFLECTIONS

Does your team have a vision or merely a strategy?

_____

_____

_____

Is everyone aware of it? Can they articulate the vision and its purpose?

_____

_____

_____

Were they part of the vision setting? Was there buy-in? If not, why not?

_____

_____

_____

COMMUNICATES EFFECTIVELY AND OPENLY

There are no facts, only interpretations.

Nietzsche

The leader communicates even when silent. Everything leaders say, do, or write impacts their credibility and their followers. The impact is seen in everything, verbal and non-verbal, including appearance. It all counts. The spirited leader takes control and strives to communicate effectively and openly. This effectiveness is measured by how well the team members' understanding matches the leader's intent.

Spirited leaders are able to be effective because they can answer "yes" to the following:

Am I willing to do my best?

Am I competent?

Do I care about the relationship with my team members?

Am I going for WIN/WIN?

Do they trust me?

Do I trust them?

The leader additionally remembers that meaning is not derived from what is said; in fact, words have much less impact than other forms of communication. Meaning is derived 55 percent from body language, 38 percent from tonality, and 7 percent from words.

The spirited leader sees communication based less in intellect and more in truth, trust, respect, and acceptance of others. The more that leaders care, the more likely they are able to influence and lead.

REFLECTIONS

How effective are your current communications? Do they add to or diminish your credibility?

_____

_____

_____

List three actions, words, or phrases you could eliminate or add that could increase your credibility tenfold.

_____

_____

_____

If you do not know, ask the people you lead . . . they do.

_____

_____

_____

FACILITATES

Wherever the sage is, he teaches without words.
Lao Tzu

A leader facilitates others' learning and unfolding of their path to self-discovery. Facilitates means "to make easy." A leader who facilitates rather than instructs acknowledges the intelligence and worth of the individual. This leadership characteristic creates a bond of trust, understanding, and mutual respect.

Facilitation encourages two-way communication. The dialogue allows for open, participative sharing, which encourages the heart. Think back . . . isn't the tonality of the speaker different and more inviting when one is asking questions to gain understanding?

By asking questions, the leader begins to understand the frame of reference, the logic, and thought process. With the intent to understand, the follower feels valued and is more receptive to the results of the communication. As a result, the team member has more understanding and ownership.

Through this process, leaders gain insight that enables them to better manage and lead. Facilitation provides the benefit of the doubt and makes fewer assumptions. Even though this exercise initially requires time, the results are long-term time and energy savings.

People who are constantly being told what to do stop listening and can become apathetic or angry. Slowly but surely their spirit retreats.

Facilitation empowers, enables, and leads. It nurtures a sense of team and community. Facilitation encourages people to reach their own truths.

REFLECTIONS

Do you tend to direct or guide?

_____

_____

_____

Are you always in a hurry and never have enough time?

_____

_____

_____

Do people often come to you for answers?

_____

_____

_____

ENCOURAGES PROBLEM-SOLVING

A problem is a chance for you to do your best.
Duke Ellington

The spirited leader believes that the people and their brain capacity are the competitive edge. Technology and equipment are merely equalizers.

Through problem-solving, the mind develops and expands, enabling intellectual capacity to build and provide advantage. The leader supports problem-solving at all levels of the organization. These leaders believe it is better to analyze and solve the situation at the level it occurs.

The leader also admits that delegating problem-solving to a person without prior experience can position a person to fail. And initial failure can undermine the confidence of the neophyte.

Consequently, leaders adapt their styles to meet the team members' competence and their exposure to problem-solving, which creates a bond of trust in which neither the leader nor the follower are disappointed.

Problem-solving taps the creative spirit and expands the mind. Problem-solving at the level it occurs fosters ownership and commitment to the solution. Solutions are implemented with less resistance, more understanding, more effectiveness, and in less time.

REFLECTIONS

Are you *the* problem solver? How does that serve you or the organization?

_____

_____

_____

Is problem-solving occurring at the level it is happening?

_____

_____

_____

Have you provided the tools, resources, and knowledge for them to solve the problem? Are people responsible for their learnings?

_____

_____

_____

RUNS INTERFERENCE AND REMOVES BARRIERS

The more I help others to succeed,
the more I succeed.
Ray Kroc

The leader is committed to cultivating an environment of learning and success. This environment is one in which helping people is rewarding, not an inconvenience.

The spirited leader intervenes when necessary without usurping a group member's credibility or authority. When made aware of roadblocks, the leader begins a dialogue.

The spirited leader seeks to understand the situation before jumping in and removing one roadblock while perhaps creating another. By asking questions and being a facilitator, the leader acquires problem-solvers, not problem-finders. With continued dialogue, the leader takes ownership for roadblocks that are beyond others' scope or capacity at the time.

The spirited leader is available to help others succeed and gain confidence. Spirited leaders take ownership for not being the roadblocks themselves.

REFLECTIONS

Do people view you as a resource or hindrance?

_____

_____

_____

What barriers currently exist that retard the growth of the team members? The organization? Are there outdated policies, reports, or procedures? Is there market research? Do they understand and know the customer and their needs?

_____

_____

_____

Would brainstorming with your group members help?

_____

_____

_____

GIVES ADEQUATE LEAD TIME

The slow, the silent power of time.

JCF von Schiller

Providing adequate lead time whenever possible is characteristic of a pro-active leader. This type of leader cares not only for the results but also the process.

With adequate time, the learning process is less stressful for the team member. Thinking back to when I was a leader, in most cases I had a project in ample time to give to someone else to share responsibility. However, the need for control would sometimes keep the project in a pile until it was panic time. Not only does this frustrate the person to whom the project has been delegated, but the manager also may feel badly that they are unable to complete all the work and, additionally, have unwittingly set up a team member for possible failure.

When leaders give their team members adequate lead time, a person can ask questions along the way, check for understanding, and do a better job. In a state of panic, important information is often forgotten.

Giving a person adequate lead time honors them and creates an environment for success. It allows the team member time to be creative, to problem solve, and to learn. It increases their chance for success, building up their confidence to take on more challenging assignments.

Giving adequate lead time also builds the leader's credibility as a person who has a handle on the business.

Providing adequate lead time whenever possible is a WIN/WIN for all: the leader, the team, the project, and morale.

REFLECTIONS

Do you consider yourself pro-active or a firefighter? Are you addicted to the sense of urgency? The visibility?

_____

_____

_____

What is in your way of becoming more pro-active and visionary?

_____

_____

_____

List three actions you can take today to become more effective.

_____

_____

_____

PROVIDES FEEDBACK

Feedback is the breakfast of champions.
W. Tate

The spirited leader views feedback as food for the soul . . . for champions. These leaders feel like champions and acknowledge the champion in everyone. Feedback is seen as a tool for growth and nourishment; it is seen as an opportunity to help guide and is considered an honor to provide.

Feedback is essential for gaining trust and recapturing spirit at work. With constructive feedback, the spirited leader provides corrective feedback, not negative or critical analysis. The difference between constructive feedback and negative analysis is that one is used for illumination, the other to diminish.

The spirited leader's intent is always for illumination and light. Thus, before providing feedback that could be hurtful, the leaders analyze their own intent. They question whether they are providing this feedback out of love and service or out of ego? With good intent, the feedback is easier to deliver and most often received with appreciation. In general, people have a deep desire and interest to know how they are doing, where they stand and how can they improve.

In addition to good intent, the leader provides corrective feedback that is clear and specific. The leader asks questions to gain and seek understanding. They focus on behavior and improvements. The leader avoids assumptions and judgments.

When providing positive feedback, the leader is again specific. They focus on behaviors and share their feelings of pride.

All feedback is given compassionately and in a timely manner.

REFLECTIONS

Do you criticize or offer constructive feedback?

_____

_____

_____

Do you listen and ask questions before giving your input to gain understanding of others' frame of reference? Do you give them the benefit of the doubt? Do you ask or attempt to determine your role in the situation occurring?

_____

_____

_____

If the answer is yes, you're probably providing feedback. If not, could you begin using these skills?

_____

_____

_____

When was the last time you gave sincere praise? What was the reaction? How did you feel?

_____

_____

_____

Is Decisive and Courageous

*Only those who risk going too far can
possibly find out how far to go.*
T. S. Eliot

People want to be led by decisive and courageous individuals. They want to be led by individuals who will not sway from their values and who make decisions based on truths.

Team members admire and respect leaders who take in information, ask questions, listen, and then take action. These leaders take calculated risks based on good judgment and common sense. They are decisive in the midst of ambiguity, are admired and respected, and at times make unpopular decisions for the highest good of everyone.

Leaders who can back up their decisions are trusted.

Decisiveness inspires and fosters confidence in the future. The spirited leader can be decisive and make difficult decisions for good reasons. Spirited leaders have faith in themselves and their team members. They have knowledge and faith in their intent. They can be courageous and go forward because failure does not exist, only learning and experiences.

With courage, the spirited leader faces and shapes the future confidently. With courage, those they lead embrace the future.

REFLECTIONS

Do people view you as autocratic? Decisive? Wishy-washy?

_____

_____

_____

Do you delegate the "hard stuff" to others to convey? Or do you willingly take responsibility and, when appropriate, explain?

_____

_____

_____

Do you model optimism for the future?

_____

_____

_____

ENCOURAGES RISK-TAKING

Mistakes are the portals of discovery.
James Joyce

Because spirited leaders are courageous and risk-takers, they encourage similar behavior from their team members. They trust their team, their abilities, and their intent. Spirited leaders know that great learning comes from first-hand experiences. Leaders enable others to grow by becoming guides and mentors to them.

Risk-taking at all levels of the organization is viewed as healthy, good, and necessary. Leaders avoid large risks by setting parameters and boundaries, while also serving as a coach. Leaders set up their group members for small successes along the way to inspire confidence and courage, while at the same time protecting the organization.

Spirited leaders realize that without risk-taking and problem-solving there is no true sense of ownership. The more ownership they feel, the more spirit that is released within and among the team members.

REFLECTIONS

Are you the defender of the status quo?

_____

_____

_____

Do you negate new or possibly outrageous ideas?

_____

_____

_____

Are you energized by risk? Or wary of most risk?

_____

_____

_____

Do you trust your staff's talents? Their thought processes? Do you understand their logic?

_____

_____

_____

USES HUMOR

A cheerful heart is a good medicine.
Proverbs 17:22

Good-natured humor is food for the soul. The spirited leader uses humor to uplift and never at another's expense. The leader sees humor as healthy and a wonderful way to defuse stress and regain perspective on a situation. Humor is a gentle reminder not to take ourselves so seriously and provides a safety valve.

Fun-loving humor is motivating and opens the lungs and heart. Remember your last chuckle? How did you feel? Lighter? Happier? More energized?

Humor uplifts and energizes and helps maintain a sense of perspective.

REFLECTIONS

Are you light-hearted but sincere about life? Do you trust yourself? Others? The universe?

_____

_____

_____

Are you serious? Are you in a trance?

_____

_____

_____

Which outlook uplifts and energizes? Which outlook tends to create stress and angst?

_____

_____

_____

MOTIVATES AND FOSTERS A CLIMATE FOR SUCCESS

We fail to recognize that people are motivated by
a need to create and a desire to serve worthwhile ends.
Joseph Badaracco, Jr. and Richard Ellsworth

Motivation is a natural byproduct of the spirited leader. The leader has fostered a culture in which motivation is inherent. This culture is one in which trust, information, opportunity, involvement, guidance, and ownership are present.

Spirited leaders are motivating because they care about the team members, the process, and the results. They ask questions and better understand their team members' frames of reference. As a result, their communications are more effective.

Spirited leaders openly share all information. They believe in and trust their followers to do their best and to be motivated. The spirited leader appreciates and respects their group members' contributions and expertise, which are their true gifts. They work in an environment of continual dialogue and facilitation for growth. With their passion toward work and people, spirited leaders ignite the passion within their group members.

The spirited leader motivates by caring, openly communicating, trusting, involving others, valuing differences, accepting, and being truthful and enthusiastic.

REFLECTIONS

Do you care about the people you lead, not just their work efforts?

_____

_____

_____

Is everyone aware of the vision and values? How they fit into the big picture? Was there buy-in?

_____

_____

_____

Do you openly communicate? Do you plan for your group members' development?

_____

_____

_____

Have you asked each individual what motivates them or have you made assumptions?

_____

_____

_____

CELEBRATES ACCOMPLISHMENTS

When someone does something well, applaud.
You'll make two people happy.
Samuel Goldwyn

Celebrating is a joy for the spirited leader. The spirited leader delights in being able to celebrate the fruits of hard labor and spirit. Celebration uplifts the spirit and replenishes the soul.

Celebration marks a passage to the next level of development, creation, innovation, and achievement. Celebration is yet another way spirited leaders demonstrate their appreciation to the people who made it happen. Celebration sparks a sense of togetherness and community.

Celebration can mark the end of a project, the launching of a new product or service, or just the desire to celebrate working together as a team. It can be helpful in acknowledging milestones, to regain momentum, and encourage the spirit.

Celebration and the resulting camaraderie, fun, stress release, and acknowledgment are food for the spirit. Celebrating can be spontaneous or planned. It is a wonderful resource during change: celebrating the future while showing appreciation for the past.

Spirited leaders can find many opportunities to celebrate and encourage, such as anniversary dates, jobs well done, new ways of doing things, new standards of quality, and productivity.

Celebration says, "Your efforts have been acknowledged. Your efforts were better than enough. You are good enough." Spirit soars and replies, "I've only just begun."

"Trust me, celebrate me and we can fly!"

REFLECTIONS

List ways you have celebrated past achievements. How often have the celebrations occurred? What were the results?

_____

_____

_____

Think of at least two reasons to celebrate today.

_____

_____

Brainstorm 10 new approaches for celebrating.

_____   _____

_____   _____

_____   _____

_____   _____

_____   _____

CONFRONTS ISSUES

That which does not kill me makes me stronger.
Nietzsche

Leaders who confront the issues earn respect. People admire individuals who are willing to confront the uncomfortable. Addressing issues tends to be uncomfortable because of the possibility for hurt feelings, defensiveness, anger, or denial. Yet leaders look past that to the positive outcomes of conflict. Leaders view conflict as good and necessary.

Conflict provides opportunities for improvement, creativity, inventiveness, and understanding. The spirited leader confronts issues in a manner that preserves human dignity and spirit. They do it with maturity and a problem-solving approach. Leaders are always looking for the lesson.

Spirited leaders know that not addressing issues can sabotage their credibility as well as drain the energy of the team. Mishandling conflict can repress the soul and lower morale.

Leaders have the wisdom and insight to know that issues and conflict are gifts from God. These gifts provide invaluable information for the good of the team, the organization, and its success.

REFLECTIONS

Do you confront issues? If not, why?

_____

_____

_____

What is your manner when confronting?

_____

_____

_____

Do you view this confrontation as a positive or negative process? Why?

_____

_____

_____

LEADS CHANGE

We must be the changes we wish to see in the world.
Gandhi

The spirited leader is a champion of change. Change fosters self-discovery and is the bedrock of a learning organization, as well as the foundation for continuous improvement and innovation. The leader is change-friendly and embraces new ideas with an open mind, free of bias, judgment, and history. Although spirited leaders embrace change, they do not keep their group members in a constant state of upheaval just to invoke change.

The spirited leader replaces upheaval with changes that make sense. These changes can be explained and discussed so that others understand the global significance as well as their personal connection to the change.

When leaders encourage support and understanding for the change, the team becomes less resistant and is free to be more exploratory. As leaders guide their group members through the transition, they focus on the outcome and the bright future. They also provide reference points and benchmarks.

Leaders keep two-way communications flowing. They praise their group members for their current skills and voice confidence in their abilities to adapt and grow with the change.

With courage, confidence, and sound business judgment, spirited leaders direct change with open sharing of information, dialogue, and encouragement. The group members are then able to become champions of change themselves.

REFLECTIONS

What is the difference between a champion of change and a change agent?

_____
_____
_____

Are you excited and 100 percent committed to necessary change?

_____
_____
_____

Do your team members understand the need for the change? Have you gained their support?

_____
_____
_____

Do they understand their role and how they fit in?

_____
_____
_____

Spirited
LEADERSHIP

Celebrates
Partnerships

INSPIRES SHARED VALUES

*Values are the foundation of our character and our confidence.
A person who dies not knowing what he stands for or what he
should stand for, will never enjoy true happiness or success.*

L. Lionel Kendrick

Shared values facilitate ownership and partnerships. Shared values are those ideals, principles, and attitudes by which everyone abides. These values serve as the foundation for interactions, problem-solving, and decision-making. Decisions are based on thinking and feeling, not policies and procedures. These shared values are applied within the organization, with the customer, and with the community.

In today's chaotic world, policies, procedures, and structures cannot keep pace. Shared values promote thinking, trust, and ownership, which leads to a more open and effective atmosphere for communication and problem-solving.

Shared values must be articulated and modeled. Spirited leaders must discuss these values and ensure they are understood. When leaders model these values, their group members follow the direction. As always, leaders should choose their words and actions wisely.

REFLECTIONS

Does your organization run by policies and procedures? Or do the people govern themselves and make decisions based on shared values?

_____

_____

_____

If they govern by values, what are these values? Are they serving the organization? Does your work environment have unwritten ground rules or double standards?

_____

_____

_____

Were these values consciously chosen or did they evolve over time?

_____

_____

_____

Are these values formalized and articulated whenever the opportunity arises?

_____

_____

_____

INVOLVES OTHERS IN THE PLANNING

Tell me, I'll forget. Show me, I may remember.
But involve me and I'll understand.

Chinese Proverb

The servant leader thrives on ownership and pride and the resulting effect on spirit. Consequently, the leader involves people in the planning process.

This strategy makes good sense because the people actually performing the work bring insight and expertise to the application. The concerns they raise and the questions they ask are blessings. The planning process is the crucial period to evaluate risks, assumptions, and resource availability.

By involving others, leaders obtain buy-in for their ideas. Team members accept that which they have a part in creating; they are more committed to its success.

Think back to a time when you felt a project was forced on you to implement and you had no input. What was your commitment? Your energy level? With buy-in, team members are less resistant to change and more committed.

Embracing change promotes innovation—the competitive advantage.

REFLECTIONS

Are your team members following you willingly? Or is there the tendency to follow you because they should?

_____

_____

_____

Do you lead or manage? Control or guide? Is it situational?

_____

_____

_____

INFLUENCES OTHERS

Since I will be no one's slave,
I will be no one's master.
Abraham Lincoln

The servant leader chooses to influence others, not control them. They feel no need to control since they believe in their group members. They believe in their inherent goodness, their desire to be their best and their willingness to accomplish the vision.

Leaders influence and gain commitment by continually being a source of information and encouragement. They influence others through their role as a leader and their well-earned credibility. They influence by listening and persuading, never with the intent to manipulate.

Manipulation is toxic to the spirit. It creates angst, self-doubt, hard feelings, and mistrust. Influencing, on the other hand, results in understanding, pride, and ownership.

A leader of influence is followed because of who they are, not because they hold a position or title. They are gracious and well-networked.

REFLECTIONS

Who usually attends your planning meetings? Are the people who are directly impacted in attendance?

_____

_____

_____

Are concerns welcomed or squelched? Do your group members feel they can be truthful? Are alternative plans considered?

_____

_____

_____

How much resistance occurs when you are implementing plans?

_____

_____

_____

THRIVES ON RECEIVING FEEDBACK AND INPUT

The very existence of the state depends on reciprocity...
it is the exchange that binds men together.
Aristotle

The spirited leader thrives on feedback and input. Feedback provides the basis for possible adjustments. Feedback helps leaders make realistic assumptions. Being open to feedback implies that leaders are aware of their humanity; they recognize that they cannot do it all alone. Accepting feedback demonstrates that leaders value their teammates and their contributions. Leaders cannot successfully serve if there is only a monologue.

Leaders must actively seek feedback and ensure the feedback process is non-threatening. Within this process, leaders truly listen to the feedback without becoming defensive. Leaders should ask questions for clarification and understanding. They then should be responsive and explain the actions they plan to take. If leaders choose not to take action on the input, they should provide an explanation, which will foster understanding and closure.

A spirited leader solicits and gives thanks for the feedback. Through their example, these leaders teach the value of two-way communication.

REFLECTIONS

Do you solicit feedback on your performance and your decisions?

_____

_____

_____

Do people freely approach you with their concerns and feelings?

_____

_____

_____

Do you listen with the intent to understand? Or do you try to rationalize and negate?

_____

_____

_____

IS A STRATEGIC THINKER

Leadership is about striving for, it's about anticipating, it's about reaching, it's almost a yearning, and creating a sense of opportunity.
Will Rapp

Spirited leaders are respected and admired for their ability to balance the short-term well being of the organization with long-term growth and stability. The leader provides the vision and enlists others to define the critical success factors and objectives to achieve the vision. The enlistment cascades to all levels of the organization to ensure that the necessary goals are tackled and achieved. Goals are mutually set and understood by all.

Although leaders focus on the long-term strategy, they are not myopic. The spirited leader and the entire organization of creative thinkers are together always searching for new opportunities and practices that support the organization and the community.

While being focused yet flexible, this spirited environment is able to adapt to new opportunities while balancing current and future needs.

REFLECTIONS

Are you one step ahead of the competition? Or playing catch-up?

_____

_____

_____

Do you consciously and consistently scan the environment for trends and patterns? Encourage others to do the same?

_____

_____

_____

List what your group is really good at doing.

_____

_____

_____

In what ways could you possibly transfer these qualities and talents?

_____

_____

_____

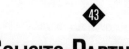

Solicits Partnerships

*Independence? We are dependent on
one another, every soul of us on earth.*
George Bernard Shaw

Partnerships grow and thrive in an environment where respect and trust are bountiful. In this type of environment, leaders honor everyone and believe in people's goodness and talents. They believe that everyone is necessary to create the whole.

True partnerships reflect 1+1=3: We are stronger, better, and more resilient together than apart.

In this environment, team members care about each other, the business, and the customer.

REFLECTIONS

Within your group, are partnerships valued?

_____

_____

_____

_____

What partnerships currently need attention?

_____

_____

_____

_____

Does your core believe that 1+1=3? List examples.

_____

_____

_____

_____

Which mentality are you modeling . . . abundance? scarcity?

_____

_____

_____

_____

CAPITALIZES ON DIFFERENCES

*With great respect and love,
I welcome you all with all my heart.*

Chidvila Sananda

The spirited leader sees the divine in everyone. Differences are valued and embraced. Differences create a more expanded view of reality and success. Differences become strengths. The servant leader capitalizes on the strengths of all. The greater the all, the greater the possibilities for creativity, synergy, and innovation.

Spirited leaders honor the sacred in each and every individual. They cherish diverse styles, talents, and abilities. As a result, the tapestry of the organization is deeper and richer. As spirited leaders validate, involve, and maximize the differences and strengths, the group experiences increased understanding and appreciation of others and their humanity.

As group members feel understood and their uniqueness is validated, they are more open to seeing differences in a positive rather than threatening manner. And when group members go beyond focusing on the differences, they become aware that we are more alike than we are different.

REFLECTIONS

What differences currently exist in your organization? Go beyond culture and race and list them.

_____

_____

_____

Identify the special gifts each one listed contributes to the organization. Consider acknowledging them and saying "thank you."

_____

_____

_____

Identify ways and opportunities to capitalize on the strengths to create a greater sense of community and appreciation.

_____

_____

_____

SEEKS COLLABORATION

We ought to think that we are one of the leaves
of a tree and the tree is humanity. We cannot
live without the others, without the tree.
Pablo Casals

Collaboration replaces competition in the spirited environment. Collaboration exists when group members experience trust and clarity of purpose. Collaboration is synergy at work where 1+1=3.

Collaboration is a key component in the learning, thriving organization. Collaboration implies seeking the highest outcome. This outcome is based on listening, dialogue, and commitment to the larger picture. It is an outcome where group members buy into the implementation, rather than merely cooperating.

Collaboration is more than cooperation. Collaborative works are active and generate ownership. A collaborative attitude reflects power to achieve the unachievable and to instill confidence and pride.

A collaborative spirit sees the interrelatedness and value of all the functions and people. It views everyone as equal and invaluable. It fosters healthy relationships and open communications. It promotes "teaming" in a true and more encompassing sense to include the entire group.

Collaboration and the sense of oneness distinguish spirited organizations. And the rewards are more than profits, they are the rewards of spirit.

REFLECTIONS

Do people at your work seek the highest outcomes or settle with compromise?

_____

_____

_____

Does everyone feel part of the whole or are they loyal to their department or division?

_____

_____

_____

Do your structure, policies, and rewards foster internal collaboration or competition?

_____

_____

_____

Identify specific changes that could be made to encourage collaboration.

_____

_____

_____

BUILDS HEALTHY RELATIONSHIPS

Leadership is a dialogue; not a monologue.
Kouzes and Posner

The spirited leader believes in building relationships: healthy relationships based on mutual trust and respect and relationships grounded in shared values, forgiveness, compassion, and honesty.

Healthy relationships exist when expectations are understood. Expectations are expressed through continual dialogue that seeks to understand the other's frame of reference, perception, and attitudes. With deep-felt understanding, the leader is better able to serve and to help the individual grow and unfold to newer heights. Once that occurs, the mission and group is served.

Through continual dialogue, balance develops between task and process and task and relationship, which creates ownership, commitment, and innovation.

Healthy relationships equal healthy businesses. Healthy businesses equal healthy profits!

REFLECTIONS

Are team members aware of your expectations? Is there clarity?

_____

_____

_____

Have you asked your group what their expectations of a leader are? Do you care what their expectations are?

_____

_____

_____

When was the last time you engaged in a conversation that did not have a specific work purpose?

_____

_____

_____

Would you characterize most of your relationships as healthy, meaningful, or toxic?

_____

_____

_____

Spirited LEADERSHIP

Instills a Sense of Community

INSTILLS ETHICAL AND MORAL ACTIONS

Greatness is not found in possessions, power,
position, or prestige. It is discovered in goodness,
humility, service, and character.

William Arthur Ward

At the core of trusting relationships and a healthy environment is moral and ethical conduct. Without morals and ethics, trust and spirit cannot develop.

This demand, though, is not one of piousness or judgment. It is about liberating spirit, giving others the benefit of the doubt, and modeling a better way.

Some people do not know a way other than ambition at any cost and losing the soul. It is through watching others with a healthy spirit that we are able to understand that morals and ethics belong at work. For me, this understanding was transformative because of the kindness and generosity of those who were willing to teach and model, who encouraged but did not judge me.

By their light, my light now shines for others.

God bless their souls for their compassion, kindness, and lack of judgment while insisting on ethics and moral conduct at all times.

REFLECTIONS

Is there a difference between ethical and moral conduct? Is one inclusive of the other?

_____

_____

_____

List your operating norms and standard practices in regard to ethics.

_____

_____

_____

What is your personal code of conduct?

_____

_____

_____

EXUDES HOPE

Hope arouses, as nothing else can arouse,
a passion for the possible.
William Sloan Coffin, Jr.

Exuding hope is a critical success factor. Usually, critical success factors refer to the nuts and bolts of what must be done for the mission to be accomplished. Without hope, the mission may be attained but with a toll on the spirit.

Hope provides the spark and the space for spirit. Hope is defined by the American Heritage Dictionary as "looking forward with confidence of fulfillment."

Today's environment of "survival of the fastest and best" can be overwhelming. Can we keep up with the competition? Will there be a downsizing? Why bother? Leaders must exude hope in their every thought, word, and action. By modeling hope, people themselves become hopeful. Followers can channel their energy on the task at hand and not their fear of the future.

Leaders' hope is grounded in optimistic realism and common sense. They provide the structure and information needed. Leaders smile and encourage. They paint a picture where everyone is part of the current masterpiece. They also exude hope of masterpieces yet to come.

Hope . . . harmony, optimism, persistence, encouragement.

REFLECTIONS

What attitudes and behaviors inspire hope?

_____

_____

_____

Which ones are you currently modeling?

_____

_____

_____

In what additional ways could hope be inspired?

_____

_____

_____

Has Fun

*The supreme accomplishment is to blur
the line between work and play.*
Arnold Toynbee

The servant leader models having fun and promotes having fun. When spirit is present at work, group members reflect commitment, pride, creativity, and fun. People enjoy their jobs, feel good about their sense of belonging and community, know they make a difference, and have fun in the process. They have the opportunity to smile, to laugh, and to take themselves lightly. They enjoy exploring, learning, and trying new approaches without fear of reprisal.

Spirited leaders have fun giving and sharing credit. They believe fun is nourishment for the soul. The leader realizes that when work is without joy and fun, passion dies. When passion dies, so does the incredible energy to accomplish the impossible, to achieve the heart's desire, and to be totally committed. With spirit dampened, the soul shrinks.

In a culture in which joy, fun, and spirit are alive, people are more trusting, committed, and creative. The spirited leader has made the image real. The work environment has become a safe place where fun, joy, and spirit abound. It is a place in which passion and profits are the norm.

Fun and joy are not luxuries, they are necessary for spirit to grow.

REFLECTIONS

Does your group reflect spontaneity and joy? Are you having fun?

_____
_____
_____

Are others having fun? Is there laughter? Smiles?

_____
_____
_____

Are people motivated and energized?

_____
_____
_____

If no, why not?

_____
_____
_____

BRINGS THOSE THEY SERVE TO LIFE

Take care of your employees, and they'll take care of your customers.
J. W. Marriott, Jr.

It's been said that the organization that knows its customer the best has no competition. I would add . . . and acts on that knowledge. The spirited leader builds trust and confidence in their group members to always keep a focus on the customer. They are an advocate for their interests, needs, and livelihood. The spirited leader realizes their very existence is dependent on serving the customer and serving the people who serve the customer.

Can you imagine an organization where everyone is focused on serving the customer? What would the quality be like? The service? Wow! The spirited leader creates such a place where everyone knows who the customer is—what they look like, sound like, their needs, and expectations.

The spirited leader allows everyone access to the customer—by sending them on business calls to their stores, creating focus groups, or even having the customer visit their location. The spirited leader has a life-size composite of the customer that "attends" all meetings or greets people in the lobby or break room.

The spirited leader brings the customer to life for each individual in the organization and releases energy when the connection is made. What excites you more . . . an organization or an actual person?

Business is relationships. People do their best for people. Release the energy . . . bring the customer to life! The results will be forever blessed.

REFLECTIONS

Who is the customer? What are their needs and expectations? Are they your partner?

_____

_____

_____

Is everyone as familiar with the customer as you are? Have they met a customer?

_____

_____

_____

Is listening to your customer the focus of your organization? Or are they supposed to listen to you?

_____

_____

_____

What is your current customer satisfaction level? Is that a mind read or based on the facts?

_____

_____

_____

PROMOTES WELLNESS

All that we are arises with our thoughts.
With our thoughts we make the world.
Buddha

The spirited leader promotes wellness at work. Wellness is healthy, nurturing, and grounding. It is the opposite of being toxic. Wellness is promoted in an environment where people are honored, trusted, surveyed for input, validated for their contributions, and inspired by hope. Levels of wellness continually evolve.

What's the implication to the individual? To the organization? Wellness promotes wholeness within the individual so that they feel cared for, recreated, and replenished. They feel grounded and sense their interconnectedness with each other. The environment reflects a sense of community.

Within the organization, wellness means less internal strife and more energy focused on the goals and vision. Wellness results in more creativity, collaboration, and innovation.

As with all behaviors, wellness has a ripple effect. It produces a positive effect on the community by people who feel a sense of well-being.

The spirited leader promotes and embodies wellness. Wellness heals the heart, the organization, and the community.

REFLECTIONS

Are you healthy physically? Emotionally? Spiritually?

_____

_____

_____

Do you have balance in all three areas of your life? Is work all-consuming?

_____

_____

_____

Do you insist on vacations? Encourage a personal life? Or a 60-hour workweek?

_____

_____

_____

Is your environment toxic or healthy?

_____

_____

_____

INSTILLS A SENSE OF COMMUNITY

We are one people, one planet.
Ambika Wauters

The spirited leader embraces oneness. In spite of the differences leaders might see, they know everyone is from the One Source. In seeing with the heart, differences melt away and oneness is apparent. As leaders treat one, they treat all as part of society.

Every action has a reaction or consequence. By bringing spirit and healing to the workplace, the community is healed. As the community and social good are promoted, the planet is healed.

Spirited leaders are devoted to a planet where trust, love, commitment, and compassion are the standard operating norms. The spirited leader visualizes such a happening. In believing so, the leader takes responsibility for each and every thought, word, and deed, knowing that healing begins with the self.

Spirited leaders are devoted to being a source of light and spirit. They honor and bless each person and situation. They believe that if their business practices serve the community, profits will follow.

Respect begets respect. Confidence creates confidence. Reap what you sow.

The gifts of trust, compassion, and a collaborative spirit reap the rewards of creativity, commitment, and innovation. Creativity, commitment, and innovation reap increased morale, reduced cycle times, increased productivity, more effective use of resources, stellar customer service, and healthier profits. An organization that flourishes and thrives amid a chaotic business environment and surpasses its competition.

Sow much, reap much. God bless your journey.

REFLECTIONS

Are you truly conscious of the impact of your words and actions on yourself? Others? The community?

_____

_____

_____

Do you care as much for the community as yourself?

_____

_____

_____

Identify three attitudes and behaviors that will instill a greater sense of community, caring, and compassion.

_____

_____

_____

How best can you serve?

_____

_____

_____

If there are other traits, characteristics, or behaviors which build trust for you, please let me know. Additionally, any quotes that touch your heart, make you laugh, or speak truth, please forward. It would be much appreciated.

Write to Ellen Castro at:

Effectiveness Consulting
6821 W. Northwest Highway, #214
Dallas, Texas 75225

(Please enclose a self-addressed, stamped envelope so that she may reply to you.)

❖

If you are unable to order this book from your local bookstore, you may order directly from the publisher. Quantity discounts for organizations are available. Call toll-free, 1-800-264-0368.